BUILD YOUR
HOUSE UPON
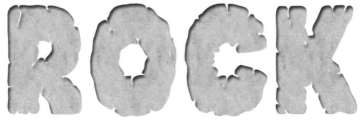

A Bible Study for Catholics
Preparing for the Sacrament of Marriage

BUILD YOUR HOUSE UPON ROCK

A Bible Study for Catholics
Preparing for the Sacrament of Marriage

NANCY HUMES

EMMAUS ROAD
PUBLISHING

Steubenville, Ohio 43952
A Division of Catholics United for the Faith
www.emmausroad.org

Emmaus Road Publishing
827 North Fourth Street
Steubenville, Ohio 43952

Library of Congress Control Number: 2012944743
ISBN: 978-1-937155-84-1

Cover design and layout by: Theresa Westling

Nihil Obstat: Michael Podrebarac, Censor Librorum,
Archdioceses of Kansas City in Kansas
Imprimatur: Most Rev. Joseph F. Naumann Archbishop
Kansas City in Kansas
Date: May 16, 2012

The *nihil obstat* and *imprimatur* are declarations that work is considered to be free from doctrinal or moral error. It is not implied that those who have granted the same agree with the content, opinions, or statements expressed.

TABLE OF CONTENTS

Introduction: High Expectations

No one has ever accused God of having low expectations. Quite the opposite actually. In the pages of Scripture, Christ announces that you are to "be perfect, just as your heavenly Father is perfect" (Mt 5:48). He also says you are to love God "with all your heart, with all your soul, and with all your mind," while, at the same time, loving "your neighbor as yourself" (Mt 22:37, 39).

In those passages, as well as countless others, God lays out His plan for your life. And that plan is sainthood. God didn't die on a cross so that you could become merely a nice person. Rather, He gave His life so that you could become holy, His adopted child who images the all-perfect God of the universe in the here and now.

Again, no low expectations there.

The same can be said of God's plan for marriage. To God, marriage isn't just an institution: It's a vocation. It's a path to holiness, a path to Him. And if God is calling you to marriage, He's asking you to do more than just love your spouse. He's asking you to imitate His love for His Spouse—the Church. In other words, He's calling you to lay down your life for your spouse, to die to yourself for the sake of their salvation.

Now, chances are you won't literally have to die to save your husband or wife—which makes answering God's call that much harder. He doesn't normally ask for big, dramatic sacrifices, but rather, little, mundane ones. He'll ask you to bathe the kids when you'd rather watch the game, to listen to your spouse talk about their day when you would rather talk about yours, or to not complain about the clothes thrown lazily on the floor, or the dinner served much too late.

Making little sacrifices like that—day after day, year after year—requires great love. It also requires great virtue. A happy, holy marriage demands much more than attraction or affection. It demands patience, wisdom, prudence, and courage. It demands faith and hope.

I'll say it one more time: God expects a great deal. The good news, however, is that He doesn't expect you to do it all on your own. God will always give you the grace you need to answer His call. And if He's calling you to marriage, He will give you the grace to love your spouse as He loves His.

Nevertheless, that doesn't mean you are off the hook entirely. There's still work for you to do. And that's what this Bible study is all about. It lays out a formula for a happy, successful marriage, based on the teachings of the Catholic Church.

How to Use This Study

This study is intended to be used by individuals or couples discerning marriage, but it can just as easily be used by couples already committed to one another in the Sacrament of Marriage and looking to improve their relationship.

Over the course of twelve chapters, you'll read about what God says a good marriage requires. You'll also be challenged to reflect on your own ideas of marriage, faith, and virtue, so that you can become more aware both of that to which God might be calling you and of the hopes and fears that can help and hinder you in marriage.

In every lesson, the questions are divided into two sections. The first section simply asks for answers straight from the Bible. The second section, however, asks you to reflect on your own thoughts about the teachings outlined in the lesson. If you do this study as a couple, you're advised to do the second section on your own, then discuss your answers together.

Whatever situation you find yourself in—married, engaged, or single—I pray that through this study our Lord will open your eyes to the truth He wants you to see. I also pray that He will give you the grace, courage, and determination you need to live this most sacred of commitments.

The Cornerstone of Faith

Your relationship with God matters. It matters to Him. It matters to you. And it matters to your marriage. The closer you are to God—the more faith you have—the more grace God can give you. And the more grace God can give you, the more grace-filled your marriage will be.

The Bible (not to mention good common sense) says that choosing the wrong foundation for your house puts the whole building in jeopardy. The same goes for your marriage. It's only as strong as its foundation.

For some people, that foundation is attraction. For others, it's the fear of being alone or having no one to care for them. Others still are motivated by material needs and people's expectations. But none of those foundations can weather the storms of life that all couples face. None of those foundations will give you a marriage built to last.

There's only one foundation that will do that: Faith.

Read

1. Read Hebrews 11:1. How does the Bible define "faith"?

_____

_____

2. According to Hebrews 11:3 and 11:6, what does faith enable you to do?

_____

_____

3. What does the Bible say about the importance of a firm foundation? (See Luke 6:46–49)

_____

_____

4. Read the following passages, and then describe what Jesus does in each passage. What does Jesus say made his actions possible?

Matthew 9:2 _____

Matthew 9:22 _____

Matthew 9:29 _____

5. Read 2 Corinthians 6:14–17. What does St. Paul say about the marriage of believers and unbelievers?

_____

_____

6. In Ephesians 6:16, what does St. Paul promise faith will do for you?

_____

_____

7. What do the following Scriptures have to say about the importance of knowing your Faith?

Colossians 2:8 _____

Hebrews: 13:9, 17 _____

1 John 4:1 _____

8. Read the Catechism of the Catholic Church, nos. 1391–1393. How does the Eucharist strengthen faith?

_____

_____

9. Read the Catechism, nos. 1457–1458. How can the Sacrament of Reconciliation help you grow in faith?

_____

_____

——————— *Reflect and Discuss* ———————

1. Describe your own faith. How important is it to you? In what ways is it part of your everyday life?

2. Why do you think the Bible advises against the marriage of believers and unbelievers? What sort of problems could arise in that kind of marriage?

3. Describe the role your faith has played in your dating relationship. Is that the role you want it to play? If not, what do you think needs to be different?

4. What role do you envision faith playing in your marriage? What are some of the ways you envision living your faith together with your spouse?

HOLY COUPLES
THROUGH THE AGES ————————
St. Basil the Elder and St. Emmelia

If you're hoping the Church will one day declare you a saint (and you should be), it will help if four of your children are declared saints as well. Such was the case with St. Basil the Elder and his wife, St. Emmelia.

St. Basil was born in AD 270 to wealthy Christian parents near Caesarea in Cappadocia (modern day Turkey). The grandson of St. Macrina the Elder, Basil held true to his faith even in the midst of widespread persecution, hiding out in the wooded mountains of Pontus for seven years during the persecutions of the emperor Maximus.

In 311, Basil emerged from the woods and resumed his career as a lawyer and professor of rhetoric. He married St. Emmelia late in life—most likely in his mid-fifties—but had no qualms about starting a large family. Emmelia herself had been orphaned as a child, and as a young woman enjoyed a reputation as a great beauty. She was also praised as a woman with both a fine mind and a virtuous character.

Throughout their married life, both Basil and Emmelia were renowned throughout Cappadocia for their work with the sick and the poor. They also were renowned for their family life. During the twenty-plus years that they were married, Emmelia bore Basil ten children. Six of those children died before reaching adulthood, but the four who survived all became great saints of the early Church: St. Basil the Great (considered the father of monasticism and a doctor of the Church), St. Gregory of Nyssa (considered the father of mysticism), St. Macrina the Younger, and St. Peter of Sebaste.

After her husband's death in 349, Emmelia, with Macrina's help, continued to oversee her children's education and religious formation. After raising her last child, Emmelia, along with Macrina, founded a religious community for women in the wilderness near Annesi. Peter later joined the monastery near his mother and sister's cloister, and, as a priest, attended to the women's spiritual needs. The other two surviving sons, both who later became bishops, visited the women often and relied upon their spiritual and theological counsel.

Emmelia died in 372 at the convent she founded. Along with her husband, she soon became revered throughout the Near East. Their feast day, May 30, is still celebrated by the Italo-Greek monks of Calabria.

Loving as God Loves

ollywood loves to end movies with the hero sweeping the heroine into his arms as the camera fades to black. Most people call those kind of movies "love stories." But they aren't. At best they're romances. But love stories? Not a chance. How can they be when the movie ends before the real loving even begins?

Love, real love, is much more than romance. It's not a feeling you have or words you declare. It's a virtue you live. It's a choice you make.

Hollywood can't teach us a whole lot about what real love looks like. But the Bible can. It is a love story—the story of God's persistent, patient, faithful, and merciful love for His people. It's the story of God's persistent, patient, faithful, merciful love for you. If you want to know what love looks like, all you have to do is look to Him. He'll not only teach you how to love, He'll give you the grace to do it.

Read

1. Read John 3:16 and 15:13. What did God do for humanity that shows you what it means to love someone?

_____

_____

2. According to John 14:15, how can you show your love for God?

_____

_____

3. Read 1 John 3:18. In what way are we to love one another?

_____

_____

4. According to Romans 12:9, what must you do for your love to be genuine?

_____

_____

5. In 1 Corinthians 13:4–8, St. Paul writes about the characteristics of genuine love. On the lines below write down each virtue or vice St. Paul names, as well as its opposite. For example: Arrogant—Humble.

_____

_____

6. What does Galatians 5:13 say about how you should demonstrate love?

_____

_____

7. In Ephesians 5:33, what advice does God give husbands and wives?

_____

_____

8. Read the Catechism, nos. 1822–1823. What is the definition of charity? How are you imitating Christ when you practice charity?

_____

_____

9. According to the Catechism, no. 1889, what part does grace play in your ability to love?

_____

_____

Reflect and Discuss

1. Pick one person who you know loves you very much. How do you know they love you? Is it by words alone? If not, describe what they do that makes you feel loved.

2. What are some of the things God has done for you that have let you know He loves you?

3. What are some of the things you do to show God you love Him? Do you do as much as you could? If not, what more could you do?

4. Think back to the virtues St. Paul lists in 1 Corinthians that he says describe genuine love. How accurately do those virtues describe your love for the person you're dating or to whom you're engaged or married? Which virtues come easily for you? Which ones are more of a struggle? Why do you think that is?

> " God in His deepest mystery is not a solitude but a family, because He has within Himself Fatherhood, Sonship, and the essence of the family, which is love. "
>
> John Paul II, *Puebla: A Pilgrimage of Faith*[1]

---

1   Pope John Paul II, *Puebla: A Pilgrimage of Faith* (Boston: Daughters of St. Paul, 1979), 86.

Wiser Than Solomon

The best things in life don't come easy. Consider wisdom. Very few children possess it. Which is why they do things like run into traffic and feed the dog lip gloss. Teenagers are usually pretty short on wisdom as well. Think "sixteen-year-old with car keys." In fact, few people are truly wise until they're older. But even then, they're not wise simply because they've lived a long time, but rather because they've learned from what they've lived.

The wise have sought understanding—of themselves and others. They've also sought understanding of God. They've made mistakes like everyone, but they've learned from those mistakes. They've reflected on the ordinary and the extraordinary, and have been changed by their reflections on both.

There are great blessings for those who've acquired such wisdom, blessings in this life and the next. But if you want to acquire those blessings and enjoy them in your marriage, you can't wait until retirement to start working for wisdom. The work has to start now, today. The fruit will follow.

Read

1. According to Proverbs 1:7, what is a good name for someone who refuses to listen to God and others?

2. In 1 Kings 3:5–13, God gives King Solomon the chance to ask for anything he wants. What does Solomon say to God? What is God's response?

_____

_____

_____

3. Read John 16:13. Upon whom should you depend if you want to grow in wisdom and understanding?

_____

_____

4. According to 1 Corinthians 13:11, what does God expect of you as you grow up?

_____

_____

5. What help has God given you to attain wisdom? What other benefit comes from that help? (See Ephesians 4:11–14)

_____

_____

6. Read Matthew 25:1–13. What lesson can you learn from the parable Christ uses in that passage?

_____

_____

7. According to James 1:5, how can you gain wisdom?

_____

_____

8. According to the Catechism, nos. 1783 and 1785, why is it important to have a well-formed conscience? How can you better form your own conscience?

_____

_____

9. Read the Catechism, no. 1831. What are the gifts of the Holy Spirit? How do those gifts help you do God's will?

_____

_____

Reflect and Discuss

1. Describe an unwise decision you made in the past. Why did you make that decision? What factors contributed to your mistake? What were the consequences? What did you learn from the experience?

_____

_____

_____

2. God expects you to "put away childish things." What are some of the childish things that you think need to be put away by someone before they enter into the Sacrament of Marriage?

_____

_____

3. What are you doing to pursue wisdom? What are some things you can do as a couple to pursue wisdom?

_____

_____

4. List some examples of foolish decision-making that could put stress on a marriage. How can you avoid making those kinds of decisions?

_____

_____

HOLY COUPLES THROUGH THE AGES
St. Gregory of Nazianzus the Elder and St. Nonna

Unlike St. Basil and St. Emmelia, St. Gregory of Nazianzus the Elder and his wife, St. Nonna, weren't able to produce four saints for the Church. This Cappadocian couple only managed three. One of those three happened to be St. Basil the Great's best friend, St. Gregory of Nazianzus the Younger, and like Basil, Gregory the Younger was later declared a doctor of the Church.

The "doctor's" father, St. Gregory of Nazianzus the Elder, owed a great deal to both his wife and son. A rich landowner and a high-ranking government official, Gregory spent many years as a member of a pseudo-pagan sect that worshipped "Zeus hypsistos." Through the prayers, offerings, and arguments of his wife, however, he eventually converted to Christianity, and after only four years of zealously living his Faith was elected bishop of Nazianzus.

Not much is known about St. Nonna. Other than her birth into a wealthy Christian family, her life-long work for the poor, and her tireless efforts to convert her husband and form her children in the Faith, history has left few details. At her funeral, however, her son Gregory described her as "supremely wise" and "my Mary." In addition to her wisdom and devotion she must have been a very persistent woman, as attested to by the success of all her efforts.

At one point in her married life, though, Nonna's success with her husband did come into question. In 359, Gregory the Elder temporarily fell in with the heretical Arians, and approved the conclusions of a heretical council. Upon hearing about what his father had done, Gregory the Younger quickly intervened and brought his father back to orthodoxy.

The couple's other two children, St. Caesarius and St. Gorgonia, went on to become, respectively, court physician to the Roman Emperor Julian the Apostate and a holy wife and mother.

Both St. Gregory the Elder and St. Nonna died in 374. Devotion to the couple was spread by their son Gregory as well as by the famous early Church historian Caesar Baronius. St. Gregory the Elder's feast is still celebrated in the East on January 1 and St. Nonna's on August 5.

Ever-Faithful

I f there is one secret to being at peace in a relationship, it's trust. Envy, jealousy, suspicion—all those things eat away at the heart of love, destroying peace and destroying contentment.

When you trust the person you love, however, your heart is peaceful whether they're with you or away from you. You know they will do the right thing, not because someone is watching them, but simply because it's the right thing to do.

That kind of trust is only possible when you practice the virtue of faithfulness.

As in everything else, God gives you the perfect example of faithfulness. His love for you never wavers. His promises never go unfulfilled. He asks you to place your trust in Him, and He never disappoints. Following His example brings its own rewards, and your relationships, without fail, will be stronger and better for it.

Read

1. What does God promise in Proverbs 3:5–6?

_____

_____

2. According to 1 Corinthians 10:13, what assurance do you have in times of trial and temptation?

_____

_____

3. Read Sirach 6:6–12. Who does the Bible say you should trust? How can you learn whom to trust?

_____

_____

4. What impediment to trust is mentioned in Colossians 3:9?

_____

_____

5. According to Proverbs 12:22, what delights the Lord?

_____

_____

6. Read Proverbs 31:10–12, 29–31. What virtues make for an admirable wife?

_____

_____

7. In Matthew 5:31–32, what does Jesus say about divorce?

_____

_____

8. Read the Catechism no. 736. How does it say you can become more faithful?

_____

_____

9. According to the Catechism, no. 1646, what does marriage (conjugal love) require? Why?

_____

_____

_____

Reflect and Discuss

1. Describe some of the ways God has been faithful to you. How has His faithfulness affected your relationship with Him?

2. Has anyone ever lost your trust? Describe the situation. What were the consequences for your relationship?

3. Why does trust matter in a relationship?

4. If you were married, what are some of the ways your spouse could lose your trust? Could your trust be regained? If so, how?

> By matrimony, therefore, the souls of the contracting parties are joined and knit together more directly and more intimately than are their bodies, and that not by any passing affection of sense or spirit, but by a deliberate and firm act of the will; and from this union of souls by God's decree, a sacred and inviolable bond arises.
>
> Pope Pius XI, *Casti Connubii*[1]

---

1   Pope Pius XI, Encyclical Letter on Christian Marriage *Casti Connubii* (December 31, 1930), no. 7.

Forgive Us Our Trespasses

I n the history of movie making, writers have put a lot of foolish words into their characters' mouths. But the most foolish words of all may have been uttered in the 1970 smash hit, *Love Story.* The words?

"Love means never having to say you're sorry."

The character couldn't have been more wrong. Love very much means saying you're sorry. In fact, it usually means saying you're sorry on a daily basis. Every day, in some way or other, we all fall. We all screw up. We all say or do something we shouldn't (or don't do or say something we should), and someone gets hurt.

Accordingly, not a day should go by where you don't reflect on your mistakes and, at the very least, ask God for His forgiveness. The more you do that, along with the regular practice of Confession, the more you can receive God's mercy. And the more you receive His mercy, the more you can extend mercy to others.

That mercy is at the heart of every good marriage. As sure as the sun will rise, your spouse will mess up. So will you. If mercy is withheld, bitterness takes root. When you grant mercy, however, it nourishes the love that brought you together. Mercy creates the space that trust and intimacy need if they are to grow.

Read

1. For what does Psalm 130:3–4 say you should be grateful?

2. Read the following Scriptures. On the lines below, describe what each passage teaches you about forgiveness.

Matthew 5:23–24 _____

Matthew 6:14–15 _____

Matthew 18:21–22 _____

3. Describe the example Jesus sets for forgiveness in Luke 23:34.

_____

_____

4. What sacrament did Jesus institute in Matthew 16:18–19?

_____

_____

5. According to Matthew 7:5 and John 8:7, what must you keep in mind before you judge the faults of others?

_____

_____

6. Out of jealousy, Jacob's sons sold Joseph, their brother, into slavery. Years later, he encounters his brothers again. What does he say to them in Genesis 45:7–8 and 50:20? What can you learn from this story?

_____

_____

7. What advice does St. Paul give in Ephesians 4:32?

_____

_____

8. Read the Catechism, no. 1422. What assurance is given?

_____

_____

9. Read the Catechism, nos. 1457–1458. Describe the difference between mortal and venial sins.

_____

_____

——— *Reflect and Discuss* ———

1. Have you ever made a serious mistake for which you were forgiven? How did that make you feel? What about a serious mistake for which you were not forgiven? Describe what it felt like to have someone carry a grudge against you.

2. Do you struggle to forgive people? Why or why not? Can you forgive someone who refuses to ask for forgiveness? Why or why not?

3. Describe a situation where you had a hard time forgiving someone. How did that hurt them? How did it hurt you?

4. What are the offenses for which you would have the hardest time forgiving your spouse? How do you think that failure to forgive would affect your marriage?

HOLY COUPLES
THROUGH THE AGES ———
St. Isidore of Madrid and St. Maria de la Cabeza

Five Spanish saints were canonized on March 16, 1622. Four of those saints were either great doctors of the Church, missionaries, or founders of religious orders: St. Ignatius of Loyola, St. Theresa of Avila, St. Francis Xavier, and St. Philip Neri. But the fifth, St. Isidore of Madrid, was a simple Spanish farmer.

Born around 1080 just outside of Madrid, Isidore had neither wealth nor land to call his own. He was a tenant farmer who worked the property of a very rich and powerful man. Despite his relative poverty, however, Isidore was passionate about the Faith and attended daily Mass.

Not surprisingly, Isidore's devotion to the Mass made him less than popular with other tenant farmers, who complained that his piety was getting in the way of his work. Isidore, however, claimed that was not the case, explaining that because he made Mass his first priority, God sent angels to help him in his labors. And sure enough, when the landowner went to spy on his tenant, he saw two angels and a pair of white horses tilling Isidore's fields.

Isidore and his wife, Maria, had one child. After the child died, however, the two determined to live as brother and sister for the remainder of their marriage and devoted themselves to a life of prayer and work. Despite their own relative poverty, they never forgot those less fortunate than themselves, and always gave away a significant portion of their crops.

Isidore died in 1130 and Maria in 1135, and devotion to the pair spread rapidly. Miracles were said to occur at their grave, and King Phillip III of Spain credited his own miraculous healing from a deadly illness to Isidore's relics. At Phillip III's request, Isidore's case was presented to Pope Gregory XV in 1619 and quickly approved in 1622. One-hundred-thirty years later Pope Benedict XIV canonized Maria.

St. Isidore is considered the patron saint of farmers, and his feast day is May 15. St. Maria shares her husband's feast day and also has her own on September 14.

God's Greatest Gifts

God is the all-powerful Lord of the Universe. He is also a Father who lovingly creates and raises up children for Himself. He gives His children the ability to love, to reason, and to forgive. He also gives them the privilege of partnering with Him in the act of creating and nurturing life.

That is a tremendous gift, and it comes with tremendous responsibilities. If you're blessed with children, nothing in your life will ever be the same. What you hope for, what you worry about, and what you do from the moment you wake up in the morning until the moment you lay down at night (and often after!), will be forever changed by the lives with which He entrusts you.

That is a daunting reality. Fortunately, the Bible is full of sage advice and practical wisdom to help you navigate the world of parenting. So don't try to go it alone. Turn to the Scriptures. Turn to God's prayer warriors in heaven. And turn to God. The grace is there.

Read

1. What was the very first command God gave to Adam and Eve in Genesis 1:28?

_____

_____

2. In Psalm 127:3–5, what does God say about children?

_____

_____

3. Hannah was a holy woman who fervently prayed for a child. Read 1 Samuel 1:26–28. How did she respond when God finally granted her prayer?

_____

_____

4. What does Psalm 139:13–16 tell us about unborn babies?

_____

_____

5. Read Matthew 18:10–14 and 19:14. What do those verses tell us about the responsibility parents have to raise their children in the Faith?

_____

_____

6. What parenting advice do the following Scriptures offer?

Proverbs 13:1 _____

Proverbs 22:6 _____

Ephesians 6:1–3 _____

Hebrews 12:11 _____

Ephesians 6:4 _____

7. What instruction does St. Paul give in 1 Timothy 5:8?

_____

_____

8. According to the Catechism, nos. 2225–2226, what must parents do for their children? In what ways does paragraph 2232 say that parents' responsibilities change as their children grow up?

_____

_____

_____

9. What does the Catechism, no. 2207, teach about the importance of family life?

_____

_____

_____ *Reflect and Discuss* _____

1. What do you think about the parenting advice the Bible gives (see question 6 above)? What do you most easily agree with? Is there anything you struggle to agree with? Why or why not?

2. How would you like to live out the Faith in your home? In other words, how do you envision passing the Catholic Faith on to your children?

3. Do you agree or disagree with the Church's prohibition against artificial contraception and in vitro fertilization? Why or why not?

4. Sometimes God gives a couple the children He wants them to have through adoption. Whether or not you encounter problems physically conceiving a child, are you open to receiving children through that route? Why or why not?

> "Thus, in the sexual relationship between man and woman two orders meet: the order of nature, which has as its object reproduction, and the personal order, which finds its expression in the love of persons and aims at the fullest realization of that love. We cannot separate the two orders, for each depends upon the other. In particular, the correct attitude to procreation is a condition of the realization of love. . . . Sexual relations between a man and a woman in marriage have their full value as a union of persons only when they go with conscious acceptance of the possibility of parenthood."
>
> John Paul II (Karol Wojtyla), *Love and Responsibility*[1]

1   Pope John Paul II (Karol Wojtyla), *Love and Responsibility* (San Francisco: Ignatius Press, 1997), 226–227.

Watch Your Mouth

Words matter. God spoke the world into being with the words, "Let there be . . . " He described His words in Hebrews 4:12 as "living and effective." And still today, He allows words spoken by the priest in the Mass to transform bread and wine into His Body and Blood.

Your words matter too. They can bring joy or sorrow. They can make a person feel loved or rejected. They can heal and they can wound. There are words you've spoken, both good and bad, that people will never forget, as well as words you can never take back no matter how hard you try.

Learning how to speak slowly with love and reverence for others is one of the most important habits you can develop. And in marriage that habit can make the difference between a happy union and a miserable one. How you talk to one another and about one another, as well as how you talk to one another about others, should always reflect an understanding of the dignity every person possesses and an awareness of words' great power.

When you worship the one called the Word, how could you want it otherwise?

Read

1. For what two things does the psalmist pray in Psalm 19:14?

2. In Psalm 141:3, what does the psalmist ask God to do for him?

_____

_____

3. According to Proverbs 15:1, what powers do words possess?

_____

_____

4. What advice does Jesus give in Matthew 5:37?

_____

_____

5. Read the following Scriptures. Describe the principle of communication to which each refers.

Ephesians 4:29 _____

Ephesians 5:4 _____

Philippians 2:14 _____

2 Timothy 2:16 _____

6. What warning does Jesus give in Matthew 12:36?

_____

_____

7. Read James 3:3–8. What problem does James describe?

_____

_____

8. Read the Catechism, no. 2477. What are some of the sins you can commit with words?

_____

_____

9. According to the Catechism, no. 2479, why are those sins so serious?

_____

_____

_____ *Reflect and Discuss* _____

1. Describe one or two instances where you've personally seen or experienced words doing lasting damage. What was said? What motivated the words? How did you or the other person react? How could the situation have been handled differently?

2. Have you ever discovered that people were speaking negatively about you behind your back? Even if it were true, how did that make you feel? What was your response?

3. What are some of the reasons you've used to excuse yourself when you've spoken negatively about someone? Which of those reasons are valid? Which are insufficient? Why?

4. Do you ever speak negatively about each other to friends or family? What damage can that do? Are there ground rules you can set that will help you know when to seek another's advice about a problem you're experiencing as a couple?

HOLY COUPLES THROUGH THE AGES _____
St. Eleazar and Blessed Delphina

Neither St. Eleazar nor his wife, Blessed Delphina, had what people today would call "normal childhoods." Both were raised not by their parents, but by their parents' siblings, and both grew up not in a home but in the midst of religious communities: St. Eleazar in the monastery of St. Victor at Marseilles where his uncle was abbot, and Blessed Delphina in the French convent where her aunt was abbess.

Their unusual upbringing may explain why, after reluctantly agreeing to their marriage that was arranged by relatives, the couple determined that they would not live together as husband and wife but rather as brother and sister. Their upbringing might also explain why they devoted themselves with such intensity to serving the poor.

After his father died, Eleazar inherited his father's title—Count of Ariano—as well as his large property holdings near Naples, Italy. Although Eleazar's subjects resisted their new master, he and his wife won their affection not by violence, as Eleazar's cousins advised, but rather through kindness. Every night, the couple invited twelve peasants to dine at their table, and never complained when their guests took advantage of them. Likewise, when Eleazar was insulted by his subjects, he simply smiled. He later told his friends and colleagues, "They said even more malicious things about Christ."

Eleazar and his wife were members of the third order of St. Francis. As Franciscan tertiaries they prayed the Liturgy of the Hours, did strict penances, and regularly performed corporal works of mercy. Despite her husband's piety, however, Delphina never rested easy about his soul. One day, as he was preparing to leave on a journey for Paris, Delphina expressed concern that the wild Parisians might tempt her husband to sin. With a laugh he told her, "If God has preserved my virtue in Naples, he can surely preserve it in Paris."

The trip to Paris didn't cost Eleazar his virtue, but it did cost him his life. The Count became seriously ill while there, and died in Paris at the age of thirty-eight. After her husband's death in 1323, Delphina sold all they had, and moved back to France, where she spent her last years serving the poor. She died thirty-seven years later in 1360.

Eleazar was canonized in 1369 by his godson Pope Urban V. Delphina was beatified in 1694 by Pope Innocent XII. The couple shares their feast day, September 27, with another French saint renowned for service to the poor, St. Vincent de Paul.

Dying to Yourself

When you're single, it's easy to buy into the idea that "It's all about me." After all, there are few, if any, people to whom you have to answer. Generally, you can do what you want when you want. And because no one except maybe your boss can make demands of you, it's easy to deceive yourself and believe that you, unlike the rest of the human race, don't really struggle with selfishness.

But for most people, marriage brings an abrupt end to any self-deception in that regard. Between the demands of your spouse and your children, life becomes one endless opportunity to die to yourself. It also becomes one constant reminder of just how difficult that death actually is.

In that death, however, is an unimaginable amount of grace. When accepted joyfully, it binds you to Christ. It gives real freedom. And it leads you home.

Read

1. What does Jesus tell his followers they must do in Matthew 20:25–28?

_____

_____

2. Read Philippians 2:3–4. How does Paul say you should think of others? How are you to approach others?

_____

_____

3. According to Matthew 7:12, what action embodies the teachings of the Law and the prophets?

_____

_____

4. What promise does God make in Luke 6:38?

_____

_____

5. According to 1 Corinthians 10:24, what are you to seek?

_____

_____

6. According to Romans 14:19, how can you encourage those you love in daily life?

_____

_____

7. What does Galatians 6:2 say you must do to fulfill the law of Christ?

_____

_____

8. Read the Catechism, no. 1852. What sins are listed alongside selfishness? What does that tell you about how serious a sin selfishness is?

_____

_____

9. According to the Catechism, no. 1818, which theological virtue guards against selfishness? How does it do that?

_____

_____

Reflect and Discuss

1. What do you think are good examples of selfish behavior? How can those examples lead to loneliness?

2. What are some practical ways you can apply the lesson from Matthew 7:12 in your daily life?

3. In what way is the counsel given in 1 Corinthians 10:24 counter-cultural?

4. Why do you think selflessness is critical to a happy marriage? In what ways or areas do you still struggle with selfishness? How is this hurting your relationship? What are some ways you can start to change that?

> "Outward sacrifice, to be genuine, must be the expression of spiritual sacrifice. . . . The prophets of the Old Covenant often denounced sacrifices that were not from the heart or not coupled with love of neighbor [cf. Amos 5:21–25; Is. 1:10–20]. . . . The only perfect sacrifice is the one that Christ offered on the cross as a total offering to the Father's love and for our salvation [cf. Heb. 9:13–14]. By uniting ourselves with his sacrifice we can make our lives a sacrifice to God."

Catechism, 2100

Pursuing Purity

Y ou don't have a body. You *are* a body—a beautiful union of flesh and spirit. Which is why when you give your body to someone, you're also giving your soul to them. You're making a gift of yourself.

God's intention, from the very beginning, was for that gift to be a complete gift, with the physical consummation of marriage serving as its sign: the union of two bodies was to signify the enduring union of two souls.

Over the centuries, however, and today more than ever, people have misused that gift. They've given their bodies with no intention of giving themselves. They've used others for their own physical pleasure or to meet their own emotional needs. They've misunderstood what love really is, and given themselves to the wrong person in the wrong way. They've also given themselves too soon, before entering into a union both blessed and lasting.

The wounds inevitably left by sexual impurity can do lasting damage to individuals and to marriages. The fruits of sexual purity, however, bring lasting blessings. Which is why seeking purity is one of the best gifts you can give, both to yourself and the person you love.

Read

1. What advice is given in Proverbs 5:18–19?

2. Where does Jesus say the sin of lust begins? (See Matthew 5:27–28)

_____

_____

3. What do we learn about the responsibilities of husbands and wives in 1 Corinthians 7:2–3, 5?

_____

_____

4. Read the words of the prayer Tobias said on his wedding night (Tobit 8:1–8). For what did he pray? How did his prayer reflect his own purity of heart?

_____

_____

5. What do the following Scriptures say about the importance of purity?

1 Corinthians 3:16 _____

1 Corinthians 6:15–20 _____

6. According to 1 Thessalonians 4:3, what is God's will for every believer?

_____

_____

7. What warning does St. Paul give us in Hebrews 13:4?

_____

_____

8. According to the Catechism, no. 1643, what is the purpose of conjugal love?

_____

_____

9. Read the Catechism, nos. 2350 and 2359. What virtue are engaged couples called to practice. What is the fruit of that practice?

_____

_____

——————————— *Reflect and Discuss* ———————————

1. Why do you think the Bible places such a strong emphasis on sexual purity? What damage do sexual sins do to both people involved? What damage can sexual sins do to a marriage?

2. Explain the difference between an unmarried couple striving for purity and a couple that is simply trying to avoid going "too far." Which approach have you tended to take? What have been the results?

3. How does the culture make it difficult to remain pure, both before and after marriage? List some of the temptations it presents to men and women.

4. What are some steps you can take, both before and after marriage, to strengthen yourself and your relationship against the temptations listed above? Be specific.

HOLY COUPLES THROUGH THE AGES ——————————
Blessed Louis and Zelie Martin

As proved by the parents of St. Basil the Great and St. Gregory of Nazianzus, doctors of the Church are most easily formed in holy households. That was true in third-century Cappadocia, and it was true in nineteenth-century France, where Blessed Louis and Zelie Martin gave birth to St. Thérèse of Lisieux, one of only three women declared a doctor of the Church.

As young adults, neither of Thérèse's parents felt called to marriage. When Louis was twenty-two he tried entering the monastery of Mt. St. Granard in Switzerland, but was sent away after only a short time. Similarly, when Zelie was still in her teens, she asked permission to join the Visitation Convent at LeMans. The sisters refused.

Unsure of what to do next, they both pursued professions—Louis as a watchmaker and Zelie as a lace maker. At the urging of Louis' mother, however, the two eventually met. At the time, Zelie said she heard a voice inside her saying, "This is the husband I have destined for you." Three months later they were married.

For the first ten months of their marriage, at Louis' request, the two lived as brother and sister. Eventually a priest persuaded the couple that God was calling them to holiness through the more normal path of married love and family life. Both agreed, and over the next thirteen years conceived nine children—five who survived childhood.

Throughout their married life the Martins' routine revolved around the parish church in Alçenon, where they attended Mass every morning at 5:30. Family prayers, visits to the poor, and other charitable endeavors marked their days. That routine was brought to an abrupt end, however, in 1877, when Zelie lost a long battle with breast cancer. After her death Louis moved the girls to Lisieux where he could be near family. He was wealthy enough to retire early, so he did, and devoted himself to caring for the girls.

One by one, three of his daughters left him for the Carmelite sisters. Although many people pitied him, Louis thought God gave him the greatest of honors by taking his girls. He was just preparing to say goodbye to one more daughter, Celine, when a sudden stroke at the age of sixty-four left him physically and mentally incapacitated. Celine delayed her entry into religious life, and cared for her father until his death seven years later. She finally joined her sisters in the Carmel in 1894, and the fifth Martin daughter, Leonie, entered the Visitation sisters in 1899.

Louis and Zelie Martin are buried near the basilica in Lisieux that was built in Thérèse's honor. A statue of the Little Flower stands between them. Their feast is celebrated on July 12.

The Good Steward

Scripture calls money "the root of all evil," but it doesn't call money itself evil. That's because it's not. Money is a tool. As a tool, it's neutral, neither good nor evil. It can, however, be used for good or evil.

Money can provide for your needs and the needs of your family, give help to those in need, and build up all that makes a culture whole and healthy. Or it can consume you, be wasted on unnecessary and even immoral goods, and drive a wedge between you and your spouse.

How you view money and how you use it will have a significant impact on your marriage. If you're generous, wise, and frugal, there will be peace and blessing. If you're greedy, foolish, or wasteful, there will be fear, anger, and strife. Learning how to use money the right way right now is a lesson that will bear fruit for decades to come. And that right way begins by inviting God into the process.

Read

1. Read the following Scripture passages. No matter how little or how much you have accumulated, what two truths must you always remember?

Job 1:21 _____

James 1:16–17 _____

2. What do you learn about contentment in the following Scriptures?

Proverbs 30:8–9 _____

Philippians 4:12–13 _____

1 Timothy 6:8–10 _____

3. According to the following passages, what should be your attitude toward money?

Proverbs 21:13 _____

Matthew 6:24_____

4. What does Proverbs 21:13 say are the consequences of ignoring those who are in need?

_____

_____

5. What promise does God make in Luke 6:38?

_____

_____

6. What lesson about true generosity does Jesus teach in Mark 12:41–44?

_____

_____

7. In Luke 12:48b, what warning is given to those who have been blessed with much?

_____

_____

8. According to the Catechism, no. 2536, what does the Tenth Commandment forbid?

_____

_____

9. Read the Catechism, nos. 2539–2540. What is envy? Why is it wrong?

_____

_____

Reflect and Discuss

1. Compare the culture's attitude about money to the Church's teachings. Which attitude do you find yourself adopting most often? Why?

2. Reflect on your own generosity. How important do you think it is to give to those in need? Does the way you budget your money reflect that? Why or why not?

3. Have you ever struggled with wanting more than you had? What were the consequences? If you got what you wanted, did it make you happier? Explain.

4. Being a good steward is about more than giving money away; it's also about taking good care of the resources you have. Evaluate how well you do in that regard. What are your strengths in terms of managing money and resources? What are your weaknesses? How could those weaknesses affect your marriage? What can you do to improve in those areas?

> "Like the oriental carpet weaver, the good wife must be an artist of love. She must remember her mission and never waste the little deeds that fill her day—the precious bits of wool she's been given to weave the majestic tapestry of married love."
>
> Alice Von Hildebrand,
> *By Love Refined: Letters to a Young Bride*[1]

---

[1]   Alice Von Hildebrand, *By Love Refined: Letters to a Young Bride* (Manchester, NH: Sophia Institute Press, 1989), 66.

In Sickness And In Health

There's a reason the original author of the ancient prayer to Mary, Hail Holy Queen, called this life a "valley of tears." Life in a fallen world is hard—very hard. There's illness and accidents, envy and malice, heartbreak and loss. There might be days, even years, when it seems as if God has forgotten you, and the cry of Psalm 22, the cry Christ uttered on the Cross, becomes your own: "My God, my God, why have you forsaken me."

But God never forsakes you. He is always with you, and always, in everything, "all things work for good for those who love God" (Rom 8:28). Even in the darkest hours of your life, He will be there, standing beside you, giving you the grace to endure and to grow.

As His child, you're called not only to believe in God's unfailing mercy, but also to extend that mercy to others. You're called to be near those who suffer, to walk with them as God walks with you. Answering that call and enduring the suffering that inevitably comes to every marriage, may be one of the hardest things you ever do. But it will also be one of the most important. And that's why the grace of the marriage sacrament is there for you to draw upon. That grace, not any kind of human wisdom or endurance, is what will ultimately see you through.

Read

1. What promise does God make in Psalm 34:4–9?

2. According to Sirach 7:34–35, what are your obligations to those who suffer?

_____

_____

3. What assurance does Jesus give in John 16:33?

_____

_____

4. Read the following Scriptures. What does each teach about the value of adversity?

Romans 5:3–5 _____

2 Corinthians 4:8–9_____

2 Timothy 4:7–8 _____

5. According to Galatians 6:2, how are you to care for others in times of adversity?

_____

_____

6. Read Philippians 4:13. What does Paul say about himself that you should also say about yourself?

_____

_____

7. What wise advice is given in James 4:13–15?

_____

_____

8. According to the Catechism, no. 1501, what are the two different paths down which illness can lead you?

_____

_____

9. Read the Catechism, nos. 1520–1523. What are the different benefits that can be received through the Sacrament of the Anointing of the Sick?

_____

_____

———————— *Reflect and Discuss* ————————

1. Give an example of a couple you know who has faced adversity with courage and strength, while remaining devoted to each other. Describe their situation. How has this impacted your faith?

2. Have you ever faced serious adversity? Describe the situation. How did you handle it? What did you do that helped you get through that tough time? What did others do that was helpful?

3. Looking back on the situation described above, how do you think God used your struggle to help you grow in faith? How are you different today because of that struggle?

4. As individuals and as a couple, what are some practical things you can do to help those you know who are suffering?

HOLY COUPLES
THROUGH THE AGES ——————————
Blessed Luigi Beltrame Quattrocchi and Blessed Maria Corsini

In many ways, Luigi Quattrocchi and his wife, Maria, were no different from most Italian couples. Both came from good Catholic families, loved sports and food, and opened their house regularly to friends. The couple was well educated. Luigi eventually became a lawyer and Maria a professor of education, but for their social class even that wasn't particularly unique.

What separated Luigi and Maria from other couples wasn't outward circumstances, but rather the intensity with which they lived their Faith in the midst of family life.

As a family they prayed the Rosary together every evening, did a Holy Hour on the first Friday of every month, and were consecrated to the Sacred Heart. Family retreats and even attending graduate theology courses at the Pontifical Gregorian University were all part of their normal routine. Luigi and Maria were also generous in giving both time and money to the poor. During the Second World War they turned their apartment in Rome's city center into a home for refugees.

Long before the war, in 1913, Maria was pregnant with their fourth child. The doctors, however, advised her to abort the baby. The pregnancy had been a difficult one, and the doctors gave Maria a 5 percent chance of surviving the delivery. But the couple refused. They waited instead for the birth, hoping for a miracle, but expecting the worst. The miracle was granted to them, and both mother and child, Maria and Enrichetta, emerged from the labor healthy and strong.

That daughter was the only one of Luigi and Maria's children who did not enter religious life. Their oldest daughter became a Benedictine cloistered nun, while their two sons became priests—one for the diocese in Rome and the other with the Trappist monks. Enrichetta cared for her parents until their death—Luigi in 1951 and Maria in 1965—and then took on the responsibility of keeping house for her brother serving in Rome.

Enrichetta and her brothers were still alive in 2001 when their parents were beatified by Pope John Paul II, and their relics were transferred to the Shrine of Divine Love in Rome. The reason for their beatification, explained Cardinal José Saraiva Martins, then Prefect of the Congregation for the Causes of Saints, was that they "made a true domestic church of their family, which was open to life, to prayer, to the social apostolate, to solidarity with the poor and to friendship."

'Til Death Do Us Part

In the eyes of the world, death is an ending. Christians, however, know better. We know death is actually just the beginning. It is the beginning of eternity, of a new life lived either in perpetual friendship or perpetual enmity with God.

For you, as for all, death will be the doorway through which you pass into heaven (possibly by way of purgatory) or hell. It will mark the Day of Judgment, the day where the measure of your life will be taken and either rewarded or found wanting.

No one can escape that day. It's waiting for you, although the hour, as Christ said, is not yours to know. What you can know, however, is the plan God has destined for all who remain faithful. There is no greater plan, no greater destiny than that one. And, through His mercy, its yours for the having, if you choose it—If you choose Him.

Read

1. According to Sirach 7:36, how should you live your life? How will that help you?

_____

_____

2. What does Wisdom 4:7–14 say matters more than living to a ripe old age? Why?

_____

_____

3. According to Isaiah 25:8, what will be the last sorrow destroyed by God?

4. In John 11:25, what words of encouragement does Jesus have for those who die believing in Him?

5. In John 14:1–3, why does Jesus tell you not to worry?

6. Read 1 Corinthians 15:13–14. Why does your faith depend on the truth of the Resurrection?

7. According to St. Paul, where is your true citizenship?
(See Philippians 3:20)

8. According to the Catechism, no. 1023, what is promised to those who die in friendship with God and have already been purified of sin?

9. Read the Catechism, nos. 1030–1031 and 1033–1035. What happens to those who die in God's friendship but still struggle with sin? What happens to those who die separated from God?

_____

_____

——————————— *Reflect and Discuss* ———————————

1. In our culture, many people avoid facing the reality of their own death. They live like they will not die. Why do you think that is?

2. Do you ever find yourself living that way? How? Why?

3. After you're gone, how do you want to be remembered? Are you living your life today in such a way that you will be remembered that way? Explain.

4. What changes can you make to your life today that would help you face death with more confidence and less fear? How will marriage help lead you to an eternity with Christ? Be specific.

> "Finally, Christian spouses, in virtue of the sacrament of Matrimony, whereby they signify and partake of the mystery of that unity and fruitful love which exists between Christ and His Church, help each other to attain to holiness in their married life and in the rearing and education of their children. By reason of their state and rank in life they have their own special gift among the people of God."
>
> Second Vatican Council, *Lumen Gentium*[1]

---

1 Second Vatican Council, Dogmatic Constitution on the Church Lumen Gentium, no. 11

Questions to Ask Yourself Before Marriage

- Is he a faithful, practicing Catholic? If not, is he willing to learn more about the Church?

- Is she open to having children and raising them Catholic?

- Have his parents set a good example in their dedication to marriage?

- Does she respect her parents and get along well with her siblings?

- How does he handle disappointment or criticism?

- Is she responsible in handling money or does she live beyond her means?

- Does he abuse alcohol or use drugs or have other self-destructive habits?

- Can you trust her or is she regularly unreliable or dishonest?

- Are the things you admire about this person based on strong character qualities?

- Will this person respect me by helping me pursue purity and practice chastity according to our state in life?

APPENDIX 2

Suggestions for Memorization

- The Ten Commandments: Deuteronomy 5:6,7,11–21

- The Seven Sacraments: Catechism, no. 1113

- Holy Days of Obligation: Catechism, no. 2177

- Gifts of the Holy Spirit: Isaiah 11:2–3; Catechism, no. 1831

- Fruits of the Holy Spirit: Galatians 5:22–23; Catechism, no. 1832